Appl[illegible] s 10

User Guide

An In-Depth and
Easy-to-Understand Guide to
Mastering Your New Series with
Simple Clear Explanations Learning
Made Effortless

BlueTed Editions

Contents

Introduction to Apple Watch Series 10

The Apple Watch Series 10 represents a significant leap forward in wearable technology, merging advanced health monitoring, connectivity, and innovative design. Since its inception, the Apple Watch has been a pioneer in redefining how people interact with technology, and the Series 10 continues this legacy by offering features that cater to both new and seasoned users. With a redesigned form factor, larger display, and enhanced capabilities, the Series 10 sets a new standard for smartwatches.

Overview of New Features

The Apple Watch Series 10 introduces a host of new features that elevate the user experience beyond mere notifications and fitness tracking.

One of the standout additions is the advanced sleep apnea detection algorithm. This feature uses machine learning to monitor breathing disturbances during sleep, providing users with critical insights into their sleep health. If signs of sleep apnea are detected, the watch will alert the user and offer recommendations for seeking professional advice. This development is a testament to Apple's commitment to utilizing its devices for preventive health care.

Another notable feature is the new depth and water temperature sensor, making the Apple Watch Series 10 a formidable companion for water activities. Whether you're snorkeling or swimming in the pool, this sensor provides real-time data on water temperature and depth, enhancing safety and performance. Additionally, the watch's 50-meter water resistance rating and automatic stroke detection further solidify its position as a must-have for aquatic enthusiasts.

The Series 10 also boasts an upgraded display with better off-angle visibility and an always-on mode that shows the second hand even when dimmed. This, combined with the enhanced brightness, makes it easier to read in various lighting conditions. For outdoor adventurers, the introduction of the Tides app offers tidal information and forecasts, allowing users to plan their water activities with greater precision. Furthermore, the Series 10's fast-charging capability, which allows the watch to reach 80% charge in just 30 minutes, ensures minimal downtime and maximum usability. This is particularly beneficial for users who rely heavily on their watch throughout the day and need quick, efficient charging.

What's in the Box

Apple is known for its minimalist packaging, and the Series 10 is no exception. Upon unboxing, users will find the Apple Watch itself, a magnetic charging cable, and a user manual. Depending on the model chosen, the box may also include additional accessories such as an extra watch band or a specific version of the watch tailored for specific use cases, such as the Hermès edition, which comes with unique straps and branding.

The watch is securely placed in a dedicated compartment to prevent any damage during shipping. The magnetic charging cable is neatly coiled and positioned alongside the watch, emphasizing Apple's attention to detail and commitment to providing a seamless unboxing experience. The user manual offers a quick start guide to help users set up their watch, along with safety information and warranty details.

In keeping with Apple's environmental goals, the packaging is made from sustainable materials, and the watch bands are crafted from a variety of eco-friendly options. This approach not only reflects Apple's commitment to sustainability but also offers users a range of choices to match their style and preferences.

Setting Up Your Apple Watch

Setting up the Apple Watch Series 10 is a straightforward process designed to get users up and running with minimal effort. Begin by turning on the watch by holding down the side button until the Apple logo appears. Once powered on, bring your iPhone close to the watch to trigger the pairing process. The iPhone will display a prompt asking if you want to set up the new Apple Watch. Tap 'Continue' and follow the on-screen instructions.

You will be guided through a series of steps that include choosing the wrist you prefer to wear your watch on, configuring your watch face, and setting up security features like a passcode. If you have an existing backup from a previous Apple Watch, you can choose to restore from that backup, which will automatically transfer your settings, apps, and preferences to the new watch. The setup process also includes enabling features such as Apple Pay, which allows you to make contactless payments directly from your watch, and Emergency SOS, which can alert emergency services and notify your contacts in case of an emergency. You can also customize the complications on your watch face to display the information most relevant to you, such as activity rings, weather, or upcoming calendar events.

Once setup is complete, the watch will sync with your iPhone, downloading any available apps and data. This may take a few minutes, depending on the amount of information being transferred. During this time, it's a good idea to familiarize yourself with the watch's interface and explore the various apps and features pre-installed on the device.

After the initial setup, you can further personalize your watch by downloading apps from the App Store and exploring new watch faces in the Watch app on your iPhone. The Series 10 supports a wide range of third-party apps, enabling you to tailor the watch to suit your lifestyle and needs. Whether you're using it for fitness tracking, managing your schedule, or staying connected with notifications and messages, the Apple Watch Series 10 is a versatile tool that seamlessly integrates with your daily routine.

The Apple Watch Series 10 is more than just a smartwatch; it's a comprehensive health and fitness device, a communication tool, and a personal assistant, all wrapped into one sleek package. With its innovative features and user-friendly setup process, it offers a compelling experience for both new and existing users. Whether you're diving into the depths of the ocean, managing your sleep health, or simply staying on top of your daily tasks, the Series 10 is equipped to support you every step of the way.

Design and Specifications of Apple Watch Series 10

The Apple Watch Series 10 represents a significant advancement in the design and technology of smartwatches. This model blends style and functionality, offering users a device that not only complements their aesthetic preferences but also provides robust performance across various activities. The Series 10 is meticulously crafted, incorporating new materials and innovative design elements that enhance both its durability and usability. Below, we delve into the design specifics, material choices, display options, water resistance features, and the available models to provide a comprehensive guide on what makes the Apple Watch Series 10 a standout device.

Physical Design and Materials

The Apple Watch Series 10 showcases a refined, streamlined design that is thinner and more ergonomic compared to its predecessors. This model is available in various materials, each offering unique benefits in terms of weight, durability, and aesthetic appeal. The watch case is crafted from three primary materials: aluminum, stainless steel, and titanium.

- **Aluminum**: This option is the lightest of the three and is available in a range of colors. The aluminum models are perfect for users who prioritize comfort and affordability without sacrificing strength. The aluminum used is 100% recycled, aligning with Apple's commitment to environmental sustainability.
- **Stainless Steel**: This material adds a touch of elegance and durability. It is

slightly heavier than aluminum but provides a more premium look and feel. The stainless steel models come in polished finishes that are resistant to scratches and corrosion, making them ideal for daily wear.

- **Titanium**: Known for its strength-to-weight ratio, titanium offers a lightweight yet robust alternative. It is more resistant to dents and scratches compared to the other materials and comes in a brushed finish that reduces fingerprint smudges. The titanium models also feature a new jet-black color option, enhancing their sleek appearance.

The back of the watch has also been redesigned, incorporating a single-layered sensor housing that improves comfort against the skin. This new design helps integrate the antenna more efficiently, contributing to the watch's overall thinness and improved cellular performance.

Display Sizes and Options

The Apple Watch Series 10 comes in two sizes: 45mm and 49mm, catering to different wrist sizes and user preferences. Both models feature a larger display area compared to the Series 9, allowing for better visibility and more detailed watch faces. The edge-to-edge display design minimizes bezels, providing an immersive visual experience.

- **Display Technology**: The Series 10 utilizes an LTPO (Low-Temperature Polycrystalline Oxide) OLED display, known for its power efficiency and high brightness levels. This technology enables the always-on display mode, which shows essential information even when the watch is idle, without significantly draining the battery.

- **Brightness and Visibility**: With a maximum brightness of 2000 nits, the Apple Watch Series 10 ensures clear visibility in various lighting conditions, whether indoors or under direct sunlight. The display also features improved off-angle readability, making it easier to view from different perspectives.
- **Customization**: Users can choose from a wide variety of watch faces, each customizable with complications that display real-time data like weather, activity rings, or calendar events. The new "Flux" watch face, exclusive to the Series 10, takes advantage of the larger screen and wider viewing angles, providing dynamic animations that make the watch feel more interactive.

Water Resistance and Durability

One of the standout features of the Apple Watch Series 10 is its enhanced water resistance and durability. The watch is rated for water resistance up to 50 meters, making it suitable for swimming, snorkeling, and other water activities.

- **Waterproof Design**: The watch's construction includes a sealed speaker and microphone system that prevents water ingress, ensuring the internal components remain dry even when submerged. The new depth sensor accurately measures underwater depths up to 6 meters, and the water temperature sensor provides real-time readings, both of which are beneficial for divers and swimmers.

- **Durability Enhancements**: The Series 10's front glass is made from Ion-X (for aluminum models) or sapphire crystal (for stainless steel and titanium models), both of which are resistant to scratches and impacts. This makes the watch more durable during physical activities or daily use. The titanium and stainless steel models, in particular, are designed to withstand more demanding environments, offering added protection against bumps and scratches.

Available Models (Standard, Hermès, Titanium)

Apple offers the Series 10 in several models to cater to different tastes and needs. These include the Standard, Hermès, and Titanium editions, each with unique features and styling.

- **Standard Models**: Available in both aluminum and stainless steel, the standard models are versatile and cater to a wide audience. The aluminum models are perfect for fitness enthusiasts and casual users, while the stainless steel models appeal to those looking for a more premium look and feel.
- **Hermès Edition**: The Hermès models are a collaboration between Apple and the luxury fashion house Hermès. These watches come with exclusive watch faces, luxury leather bands, and a unique branding that sets them apart from the standard models. The Hermès edition is ideal for users who value fashion and luxury in their technology.
- **Titanium Edition**: The Titanium models, available in brushed and jet-black finishes, are designed for those

who need a lightweight yet durable watch. This edition is particularly popular among athletes and outdoor enthusiasts due to its robust construction and high-end aesthetics.

Step-by-Step Setup Guide

Setting up your Apple Watch Series 10 is a seamless process designed to integrate your device quickly into your daily life.

1. **Unboxing**: Carefully remove the watch and accessories from the box. Place the watch on a flat surface and connect it to the magnetic charging cable.
2. **Power On**: Hold the side button until the Apple logo appears. Bring your iPhone close to the watch to initiate the pairing process.

3. **Pairing with iPhone**: Follow the on-screen instructions on your iPhone to pair the devices. You will see a pattern on your watch screen that you must scan with your iPhone to complete the pairing.
4. **Customization**: Choose your preferred settings for watch faces, complications, and notifications. You can also configure health and fitness tracking features at this stage.
5. **Install Apps**: Download and install any additional apps you want on your watch. Explore the App Store for apps specifically designed to enhance your Apple Watch experience.
6. **Syncing Data**: Allow the watch to sync with your iPhone, transferring data such as contacts, music, and health information. This may take a few minutes.

7. **Explore Features**: Once setup is complete, familiarize yourself with the features and settings of your new watch. Try out different watch faces and explore the pre-installed apps to get the most out of your device.

The Apple Watch Series 10 is a comprehensive device that offers something for everyone, from fitness tracking to luxury design. With its advanced features and elegant design, it sets a new standard in wearable technology.

Setting Up Your Apple Watch

Setting up your Apple Watch is an essential first step to ensure you get the most out of this advanced device. Whether you're a new user or upgrading from an older model, the setup process is designed to be simple and user-friendly. This guide will walk you through the steps for pairing your Apple Watch with an iPhone, configuring initial settings, customizing watch faces, and managing apps effectively.

Pairing with iPhone

1. **Turn on the Apple Watch**: Start by pressing and holding the side button on your Apple Watch until you see the Apple logo. Place the watch and your iPhone close together to begin the pairing process.

2. **Launch the Apple Watch App on iPhone**: Open the Apple Watch app on your iPhone. If this is your first time setting up an Apple Watch, the app will automatically prompt you to start the pairing process. Tap on "Start Pairing" to continue.
3. **Align the Watch Screen with the Camera**: A unique animation will appear on the Apple Watch screen. Hold your iPhone over the watch so that the watch face appears in the viewfinder of your iPhone camera. The devices will pair automatically. If this method doesn't work, you can select "Pair Apple Watch Manually" and follow the on-screen instructions.
4. **Set Up as New or Restore from Backup**: Once paired, you have the option to set up your watch as a new

device or restore it from an existing backup if you had a previous Apple Watch. Choose “Restore from Backup” if you want to transfer your data, settings, and apps from an old watch to the new one.

5. **Sign in with Apple ID**: Enter your Apple ID credentials to access features like Activity, Apple Pay, and iCloud syncing. This step is crucial for enabling various Apple services on your watch.
6. **Configure Basic Settings**: You will be prompted to set your preferences for settings such as location services, Siri, and diagnostics. Choose your desired settings, as these will impact how you use your watch.

Initial Setup and Configuration

1. **Set a Passcode**: For security, you will be asked to create a passcode for your watch. This passcode is necessary to use Apple Pay and to unlock the watch after it has been removed from your wrist. You can skip this step, but it's recommended for security purposes.
2. **Configure Apple Pay**: If you choose to set up Apple Pay, follow the instructions to add your credit or debit card to the watch. You can use the camera on your iPhone to capture the card information, or enter it manually.
3. **Enable Emergency SOS**: You can set up Emergency SOS to automatically call local emergency services and send notifications to your emergency contacts

if you hold down the side button on your watch.

4. **Health and Fitness Settings**: Set up health and fitness features by entering your information such as age, weight, height, and activity level. This information helps the watch calculate calories burned and other health metrics more accurately.
5. **Sync Apps and Data**: The watch will sync apps and settings from your iPhone that are compatible with the watch. This process might take a few minutes, depending on how much data is being transferred. You can customize which apps to sync during this setup step.
6. **Explore the Watch Interface**: Once the initial setup is complete, take some time to familiarize yourself with the Apple Watch interface. The Digital Crown

and side button can be used to navigate through menus, and you can access the Control Center by swiping up from the bottom of the screen.

Customizing Watch Faces

1. **Access the Watch Face Gallery**: Open the Watch app on your iPhone and tap on “Face Gallery” at the bottom of the screen. Here, you’ll see a wide variety of watch faces to choose from, including Modular, Infograph, and new faces like “California” or “Artist.”
2. **Select a Watch Face**: Tap on a watch face to see a preview and customize its appearance. You can change the color scheme, add or remove complications (data displayed on the watch face), and adjust other settings to suit your style and needs.

3. **Add Complications**: Complications are small widgets that display information from apps. You can add complications like weather, activity rings, heart rate, or calendar events to your watch face. Tap on a complication slot and select the data you want to display.
4. **Set as Your Watch Face**: Once you've customized your watch face, tap "Add" to make it your active watch face. You can switch between multiple watch faces by swiping left or right on the watch screen.
5. **Edit Directly on the Watch**: You can also customize watch faces directly on your Apple Watch. Press firmly on the watch face to enter editing mode, then swipe to choose a new face or tap "Customize" to adjust the current one.

Adding and Organizing Apps

1. **Access the App Store**: Open the App Store on your Apple Watch or the Watch app on your iPhone. Search for apps specifically designed for the watch, such as fitness trackers, music players, or productivity tools.
2. **Download and Install Apps**: Tap "Get" or the download icon to install an app on your Apple Watch. Once installed, the app icon will appear on the watch's Home Screen. You can rearrange apps on the Home Screen by tapping and holding an app icon until they all start to jiggle, then dragging them to the desired location.
3. **Organize Apps Using the Watch App on iPhone**: Open the Watch app on your iPhone, go to "My Watch," and

tap "App Layout." You can drag app icons around to organize them as you like. This layout will be reflected on your Apple Watch.

4. **Manage Notifications for Apps**: Go to the Watch app on your iPhone, select "Notifications," and choose which apps can send alerts to your watch. This helps reduce distractions and ensures you only receive important notifications.
5. **Remove Unwanted Apps**: To remove an app from your Apple Watch, press and hold the app icon until it jiggles, then tap the small "x" that appears. Confirm the deletion to remove the app from your watch.
6. **Use the Dock for Quick Access**: The Dock is a convenient way to access your favorite or most recent apps. Press the side button to open the Dock, then scroll

through your apps. You can customize the Dock to show either your favorite apps or the ones you used most recently.

By following these detailed, step-by-step instructions, you can set up your Apple Watch Series 10 to suit your preferences and make the most out of its powerful features. Whether you're new to the Apple Watch or upgrading from an older model, this guide will help you navigate the setup process with ease.

Navigating Your Apple Watch

Navigating the Apple Watch Series 10 effectively is crucial for taking full advantage of its features. This guide will walk you through the basics of using the Digital Crown and side button, managing the Control Center and notifications, exploring the WatchOS 11 interface, and mastering the new gestures and shortcuts. Whether you're a new user or upgrading from an older model, these step-by-step instructions will help you get the most out of your device.

Using the Digital Crown and Side Button

The Digital Crown and side button are the primary tools for interacting with your Apple Watch. Here's how to use them effectively:

1. **The Digital Crown:**
   - **Scrolling and Zooming:** Turn the Digital Crown to scroll through lists, zoom in and out of images, and adjust settings. For example, when you're viewing messages or emails, rotating the crown will scroll through the text.
   - **Returning to the Watch Face:** Press the Digital Crown once to go back to the watch face from any app or screen.
   - **Accessing the App Screen:** Press the Digital Crown once to open the app screen. Apps are displayed in a grid or list view, depending on your preference. Rotate the crown to zoom in and out of the app grid.

- **Activating Siri:** Press and hold the Digital Crown to activate Siri. You can then ask Siri to perform tasks such as sending messages, setting reminders, or answering questions.

2. **The Side Button:**
    - **Opening the Dock:** Press the side button once to access the Dock, where you can see your most recently used apps or favorite apps, depending on your settings. Scroll through the Dock using the Digital Crown or swipe up and down on the screen.
    - **Using Apple Pay:** Double-click the side button to activate Apple Pay. Hold the watch near a contactless reader to make a payment.

- ○ **Turning Off the Watch:** Press and hold the side button to access the power menu, where you can choose to power off, access medical ID, or activate Emergency SOS.

3. **Force Touch (Pressing Firmly):** While Force Touch is not supported on newer Apple Watch models, pressing firmly on some older models can reveal additional options. For example, you can use Force Touch to change the watch face or access hidden settings within certain apps.

Control Center and Notifications

The Control Center and notifications are key elements for managing your Apple Watch. They allow you to quickly access settings and respond to alerts.

1. **Accessing the Control Center:**
    - **From the Watch Face:** Swipe up from the bottom of the screen to open the Control Center. Here, you'll find quick settings such as Airplane Mode, Do Not Disturb, and Battery Life.
    - **From Any App:** Press and hold the bottom of the screen, then swipe up to access the Control Center while using an app. This is useful for making quick adjustments without leaving your current activity.
2. **Using Control Center Features:**
    - **Airplane Mode:** Tap the airplane icon to turn on Airplane Mode, which disables all wireless connections.

- **Do Not Disturb:** Tap the crescent moon icon to enable Do Not Disturb. This will silence calls and alerts.
- **Battery Life:** Tap the battery percentage icon to see detailed battery information, including Power Reserve mode.
- **Flashlight:** Tap the flashlight icon to use your watch screen as a light source. You can swipe left or right to switch between a standard light, flashing light, and red light.

3. **Managing Notifications:**
    - **Viewing Notifications:** Swipe down from the top of the screen to see your notifications. Scroll through them using the Digital Crown or your finger.

- **Responding to Notifications:** Tap on a notification to open it. You can then choose to respond, dismiss, or clear all notifications.
- **Customizing Notification Settings:** Go to the Watch app on your iPhone and select "Notifications." From here, you can customize which apps are allowed to send alerts to your watch and adjust how these notifications are presented.

Exploring the WatchOS 11 Interface

The WatchOS 11 interface is designed to be intuitive and easy to navigate. Here's a breakdown of its features:

1. **App Layout:**
    - **Grid View:** Apps are displayed in a honeycomb pattern. You can navigate this layout by swiping around or using the Digital Crown to zoom in and out.
    - **List View:** Alternatively, you can choose List View from the settings. This displays apps in a vertical list, which you can scroll through using the Digital Crown.
2. **Watch Faces:**
    - WatchOS 11 offers a variety of new and customizable watch faces. To change your watch face, press and hold the watch face screen, then swipe left or right to select a different face. You can also customize each face by tapping

"Edit" and adjusting the complications and colors.

3. **Notifications and Control Center Customization:**
   - WatchOS 11 allows for more control over your notifications and Control Center layout. You can add, remove, and rearrange controls such as Wi-Fi, Airplane Mode, and others according to your preferences.
4. **Focus Mode Integration:**
   - With Focus Mode integration, you can align your watch notifications with your iPhone's Focus settings. This helps reduce distractions by allowing you to only receive alerts that are relevant to your current activity or location.

New Gestures and Shortcuts

WatchOS 11 introduces new gestures and shortcuts that make navigating your Apple Watch even more efficient.

1. **Gestures:**
    - **Swiping:** Use swipes to navigate between different screens. Swipe left or right to switch between watch faces. Swipe up to access the Control Center and down for notifications.
    - **Double Tap:** Double-tap the screen to zoom in on certain elements, such as when reading text or viewing photos.
    - **Cover to Mute:** If you receive a call or notification in a quiet environment, you can quickly silence your watch by covering the

screen with your hand for a few seconds.

2. **Shortcuts:**
   - **Quick Actions:** Apple Watch now supports Quick Actions, allowing you to perform specific tasks with a double-click of the side button. For instance, you can use this shortcut to launch your favorite workout or navigate to the last used app.
   - **Assistive Touch:** This feature enables you to control your watch using hand gestures. For example, clenching your fist can simulate a tap, and pinching can move the focus between options on the screen.
3. **Siri Shortcuts:**
   - You can set up Siri Shortcuts on your iPhone, which will then be

available on your Apple Watch. These shortcuts can automate tasks like sending messages, starting a workout, or playing a specific playlist.

4. **Backtrack and Compass Waypoints:**
   - The new Backtrack feature helps you retrace your steps if you get lost. It records your path and can guide you back to your starting point. Compass Waypoints allow you to mark specific locations with custom labels, making it easier to navigate trails and explore new areas.

By mastering these navigational tools and features, you can optimize your Apple Watch experience, making it a powerful tool for both everyday use and specific tasks. Whether you're using it for fitness tracking, staying connected, or managing your day, the Series 10 offers intuitive controls and a wealth of options to suit your needs.

Health and Fitness Features of Apple Watch Series 10

The Apple Watch Series 10 is a powerful tool for monitoring and improving your health and fitness. With advanced sensors and an intuitive interface, it offers a comprehensive suite of features that help you stay active, track your health metrics, and respond to emergencies. This guide covers the key health and fitness features, including activity tracking, sleep apnea monitoring, heart rate and blood oxygen monitoring, fall detection, Emergency SOS, and using the Health app.

Activity Tracking and Goals

The Apple Watch Series 10 makes it easy to track your daily activities and set personalized fitness goals. Here's how to make the most of this feature:

1. **Setting Up Activity Goals:**
   - Open the *Activity* app on your Apple Watch. You will be prompted to set your daily goals for Move, Exercise, and Stand rings. These goals represent your calorie expenditure, minutes of exercise, and standing hours per day, respectively.
   - Adjust the goals according to your fitness level. For example, if you are just starting out, set a moderate Move goal and gradually increase it as you build your stamina.
2. **Tracking Your Progress:**
   - Throughout the day, your watch will monitor your activity and update your progress in real-time. Each ring will fill up as you achieve your goals. The Move ring tracks

active calories burned, the Exercise ring fills up with any activity equivalent to a brisk walk or higher, and the Stand ring tracks the number of hours you've stood and moved for at least one minute.

- You can view detailed stats by opening the *Activity* app on your watch or iPhone. This includes steps taken, distance covered, and flights climbed.

3. **Receiving Notifications and Encouragement:**
   - The Apple Watch provides personalized reminders and encouragement to help you stay on track. For instance, you might receive a nudge to stand up if you've been sitting too long, or a

notification celebrating your progress when you close a ring.

  - Use these notifications to adjust your activity throughout the day and stay motivated.

4. **Competing with Friends:**
   - You can share your activity with friends and family and even engage in competitions to see who can close the most rings. To do this, open the *Activity* app on your iPhone, tap the *Sharing* tab, and invite friends.

Sleep Apnea Monitoring

The Series 10 introduces a sleep apnea monitoring feature, which uses advanced algorithms to detect irregular breathing patterns during sleep. Here's how to set it up and use it:

1. **Enabling Sleep Apnea Monitoring:**
    - Open the *Health* app on your iPhone and navigate to the *Respiratory* section. You will find the option to enable sleep apnea monitoring. Follow the prompts to activate the feature.
    - You may be asked to provide some basic health information such as your age, weight, and height. This data helps the algorithm provide more accurate results.
2. **Wearing Your Watch to Bed:**
    - For accurate monitoring, wear your watch snugly on your wrist while you sleep. The sensors will track your breathing patterns throughout the night.
    - Ensure your watch has sufficient battery before going to bed. The

Series 10 features quick charging, so you can top it up before bedtime if needed.

3. **Interpreting the Data:**
   - In the morning, open the *Health* app to view your sleep data. The app will display metrics like total sleep duration, sleep stages, and breathing disturbances.
   - If the watch detects signs of sleep apnea, it will notify you and provide a report that you can share with your healthcare provider. This report includes information such as the time and duration of breathing disturbances.
4. **Taking Action:**
   - If you receive a sleep apnea alert, it's important to consult a healthcare professional. Early

detection and treatment of sleep apnea can significantly improve your overall health and quality of life.

Heart Rate and Blood Oxygen Monitoring

The Apple Watch Series 10 is equipped with sensors that continuously monitor your heart rate and blood oxygen levels. Here's how to use these features:

1. **Heart Rate Monitoring:**
    - The heart rate sensor is active throughout the day and can be accessed through the *Heart Rate* app on your watch. You can see your current heart rate, resting rate, walking average, and more.

- To take a manual reading, open the *Heart Rate* app and wait a few seconds for the sensor to measure your heart rate.

2. **High and Low Heart Rate Notifications:**
    - You can set up notifications for unusually high or low heart rates, which can indicate potential health issues. To enable these, go to the *Watch* app on your iPhone, tap *Heart*, and set your desired thresholds.
3. **Blood Oxygen Monitoring:**
    - The *Blood Oxygen* app measures the oxygen level in your blood, which is an indicator of your respiratory health. To take a measurement, open the app on your watch and keep your wrist

steady for 15 seconds while the sensor performs the test.

- Regular monitoring can provide insights into your overall wellness and help identify issues like sleep apnea or respiratory conditions.

4. **Viewing Your Data:**
   - All heart rate and blood oxygen data is stored in the *Health* app on your iPhone. You can view trends over time and share this data with your healthcare provider if needed.

Fall Detection and Emergency SOS

The Apple Watch Series 10 includes advanced safety features like fall detection and Emergency SOS, which can be lifesaving in critical situations.

1. **Enabling Fall Detection:**
   - To enable fall detection, open the *Watch* app on your iPhone, go to *Emergency SOS*, and toggle on *Fall Detection*. This feature uses the watch's accelerometer and gyroscope to detect when you've taken a hard fall.
   - If a fall is detected, the watch will tap your wrist and display an alert. You can dismiss the alert if you're fine, or it will automatically call emergency services if you remain immobile for about a minute.
2. **Using Emergency SOS:**
   - Press and hold the side button on your Apple Watch until the Emergency SOS slider appears. Slide it to call emergency services immediately. The watch will also

send your location to your emergency contacts.
    - This feature is crucial for those who may find themselves in unsafe situations or need help quickly.
3. **Updating Emergency Contacts:**
    - Make sure your emergency contacts are up to date in the *Health* app on your iPhone. Go to *Medical ID* and add or edit contacts as needed.

Using the Health App with Apple Watch

The Health app on your iPhone integrates all the data collected by your Apple Watch, providing a comprehensive overview of your health.

1. **Setting Up Health Data:**
   - Open the *Health* app and tap on *Summary*. You can set up your health profile, including information like age, weight, and medical conditions.
   - Customize the *Health Data* categories you want to track, such as heart rate, activity, and sleep. You can also add third-party apps that sync data with the Health app.
2. **Viewing Health Trends:**
   - The *Health* app provides visualizations of your data over time, making it easy to identify trends. For example, you can see how your average resting heart rate changes over weeks or months.
   - Use these insights to adjust your fitness routine or consult with a

healthcare professional if you notice any unusual patterns.

3. **Sharing Data with Healthcare Providers:**
   - The Health app allows you to share your health data with your healthcare provider. This can be especially useful for tracking chronic conditions or sharing data from specialized tests, such as ECG or blood oxygen levels.
4. **Setting Up Health Notifications:**
   - You can set up notifications for important health metrics, such as irregular heart rhythms or sleep apnea alerts. Go to the *Health* app, select *Notifications*, and choose the alerts you want to receive.

By following these steps, you can make the most of the health and fitness features on your Apple Watch Series 10, using it as a powerful tool for maintaining and improving your overall well-being.

Fitness and Workout Features of Apple Watch Series 10

The Apple Watch Series 10 is a versatile fitness companion, offering advanced features to help you achieve your workout goals and track your progress comprehensively. Whether you're a seasoned athlete or just starting your fitness journey, the built-in workouts, customizable options, and innovative new apps like Tides and Depth make the Series 10 an invaluable tool. This guide will walk you through the core fitness features, from setting up workouts to managing your data and exploring new activities like swimming and water sports.

Built-in Workouts and Custom Workouts

The Apple Watch Series 10 comes with a variety of built-in workout options, including running, cycling, swimming, yoga, and more. You can also create custom workouts tailored to your specific needs. Here's how to get started:

1. **Starting a Built-in Workout:**
    - Open the *Workout* app on your Apple Watch. Scroll through the list of available workouts, which includes popular activities like *Outdoor Run*, *HIIT*, *Rowing*, and *Strength Training*.
    - Tap on the workout you want to start. For many workouts, you can customize goals by tapping the three dots icon. You can set a target for calories, time, distance, or simply choose an open goal if you're not focusing on a specific metric.

2. **Creating a Custom Workout:**
    - To create a custom workout, scroll down to the bottom of the workout list in the *Workout* app and select *Add Workout.*
    - Choose a base workout type and then tap on *Custom* at the top of the screen. You can now set up your workout by configuring intervals, rest periods, and targets. For example, you can create a running workout that alternates between sprints and walking, with set rest times between intervals.
    - Save the custom workout for future use. You can access it anytime from the main *Workout* app menu.

3. **Using the Watch Face Complications:**
    - You can add workout-related complications to your watch face for quick access. For instance, you can add a shortcut to start your favorite workout directly from the watch face or view your current progress without opening the *Workout* app.
4. **Setting Up Personalized Alerts:**
    - You can set alerts for different metrics, such as pace, heart rate, or cadence. These alerts help you stay within your desired range during a workout. For example, if your goal is to maintain a certain heart rate zone during a cardio session, you can set an alert to notify you when you go above or below that range.

5. **Pausing and Resuming Workouts:**
   - To pause your workout, simply press the Digital Crown and side button simultaneously. To resume, press both buttons again. This is useful if you need to take a short break during your exercise session.

Using the New Tides and Depth Apps

The Tides and Depth apps are new additions to the Apple Watch Series 10, designed for users who engage in water activities like surfing, snorkeling, and swimming.

1. **Using the Tides App:**
   - Open the *Tides* app on your Apple Watch. This app provides real-time tidal information, including high and low tides, rising and falling

tides, and tide height and direction.

- Use the scroll wheel to view a seven-day forecast for tidal patterns at your favorite beach or coastal location. This is especially useful for planning activities like surfing or beach outings.
- You can set complications on your watch face to display current tidal information, making it easy to check conditions at a glance.

2. **Using the Depth App:**
   - The *Depth* app is perfect for divers and swimmers. Open the app before entering the water to activate the depth gauge and water temperature sensor.
   - The app will automatically start recording once it detects that you

are submerged. It displays the current depth, maximum depth, water temperature, and the duration of your underwater session.

- You can set depth alerts to notify you when you reach a certain depth, which is particularly useful for safety in diving.

3. **Customizing App Settings:**
   - Go to the *Watch* app on your iPhone and select the *Tides* or *Depth* app to customize settings like units of measurement, favorite locations, and alerts. This customization allows you to tailor the apps to your specific water activity needs.

Tracking Swimming and Water Activities

The Apple Watch Series 10 is built to handle various water activities, offering robust tracking features for swimming in pools, open water, and other aquatic sports.

1. **Starting a Swim Workout:**
    - Open the *Workout* app and select either *Pool Swim* or *Open Water Swim*. For pool swimming, you'll be prompted to enter the pool length. This helps the watch calculate your laps and distance accurately.
    - Tap *Start* to begin your workout. The watch will track your strokes, laps, distance, and time automatically. It can differentiate between different swim strokes,

such as freestyle, backstroke, and butterfly.

2. **Using the Auto-Pause Feature:**
    - The Series 10 can automatically pause your swim workout when you rest at the pool edge and resume when you start swimming again. This feature is useful for tracking your active swim time without manually pausing and resuming.
3. **Reviewing Swim Metrics:**
    - After your swim, open the *Activity* app on your iPhone to view detailed metrics, including your swim stroke type, lap splits, and average pace. This data helps you analyze your performance and identify areas for improvement.

4. **Water Lock and Ejecting Water:**
   - The Apple Watch Series 10 automatically activates Water Lock during swim workouts, which prevents accidental touches. To turn off Water Lock and eject any water from the speaker, rotate the Digital Crown. You'll hear a series of tones as the watch expels water from its speaker.
5. **Tracking Snorkeling and Diving:**
   - Use the *Depth* app for snorkeling or shallow diving. The watch can measure depths up to 6 meters and monitor water temperature, giving you valuable data for your underwater activities.

Managing Workout Metrics and History

Keeping track of your workout history and analyzing metrics is essential for monitoring progress and achieving your fitness goals. The Apple Watch Series 10 makes this process straightforward.

1. **Viewing Workout History:**
    - Open the *Fitness* app on your iPhone and tap on the *Summary* tab to see a detailed overview of your recent workouts. You can view data such as total calories burned, workout duration, and average heart rate.
    - Tap on any workout to see more detailed metrics, including splits, elevation gain, and heart rate zones. This information helps you

assess the effectiveness of your workouts.

2. **Using the *Trends* Feature:**
   - The *Fitness* app includes a *Trends* feature that shows your long-term progress in various fitness metrics. This includes metrics like your running pace, walking speed, and exercise minutes.
   - Analyzing trends over time can help you understand your overall fitness progression and adjust your training plans accordingly.
3. **Sharing Workout Data:**
   - You can share your workout data with friends, coaches, or healthcare providers. In the *Fitness* app, select a workout and tap the share icon to send a summary or detailed report of your workout.

- This feature is useful for accountability and receiving feedback on your training.

4. **Exporting Data:**
    - If you use third-party apps for fitness tracking, you can export your workout data from the *Health* app. Open the *Health* app, go to *Health Data,* and select *Export Health Data.* This creates a file that you can share with other apps or services.

5. **Setting Up Fitness Goals:**
    - You can set weekly goals for different fitness activities in the *Fitness* app. For example, you can aim to complete a certain number of workouts per week or achieve a specific calorie burn target. These

goals help keep you motivated and focused.

By mastering these fitness and workout features, you can make the most of your Apple Watch Series 10, transforming it into a comprehensive tool for health and fitness tracking. Whether you're swimming, running, or diving into new water sports, the Series 10 has the capabilities to support your active lifestyle.

Productivity and Communication on Apple Watch Series 10

The Apple Watch Series 10 is not just a fitness tracker but also a powerful productivity and communication tool. With features like Siri, call and message capabilities, and seamless integration with calendar and reminders, it enables you to stay connected and manage your tasks efficiently right from your wrist. This guide provides step-by-step instructions to maximize your productivity and communication using these features.

Using Siri on Apple Watch

Siri on the Apple Watch is your personal assistant that can help with a variety of tasks, from setting reminders to finding directions. Here's how to use Siri effectively:

1. **Activating Siri:**
    - **Raise to Speak:** Simply raise your wrist close to your mouth and start speaking to activate Siri. There is no need to say "Hey Siri" if this feature is enabled.
    - **Using the Digital Crown:** Press and hold the Digital Crown until you see the Siri waveform appear on the screen, then speak your command.
    - **Voice Activation:** If you have enabled "Hey Siri" in your settings, just say "Hey Siri" followed by your command, even without raising your wrist.
2. **Common Commands:**
    - **Setting Reminders and Alarms:** Say, "Set a reminder to call John at 3 PM" or "Set an alarm

for 6 AM." Siri will confirm the action and display the set reminder or alarm on the screen.

  - **Sending Messages and Making Calls:** You can say, "Text Sarah that I'm on my way" or "Call Mom on her mobile." Siri will initiate the action and show the progress on your watch.
  - **Navigating and Finding Locations:** Ask Siri for directions or information about nearby places, such as "Find the nearest coffee shop" or "What's the weather today?"

3. **Customizing Siri Settings:**
  - Open the *Watch* app on your iPhone, go to *Siri*, and configure settings such as language, voice feedback, and raise to speak. You

can also control Siri's responses and choose whether or not Siri can be activated when your watch is in silent mode.

4. **Using Siri Shortcuts:**
   - Siri Shortcuts allow you to create custom voice commands for specific actions, like starting a workout or playing your favorite playlist. Go to the *Shortcuts* app on your iPhone, create a new shortcut, and link it to a Siri phrase. This shortcut will now be accessible via Siri on your Apple Watch.

Making and Receiving Calls

The Apple Watch Series 10 can handle calls, making it easy to stay connected without reaching for your phone. Here's how to make and receive calls on your watch:

1. **Making a Call:**
   - Open the *Phone* app on your Apple Watch. You'll see a list of recent contacts and a keypad.
   - Tap *Contacts* to browse through your saved contacts or use the *Keypad* to dial a number manually.
   - Tap the phone icon next to the contact or enter the number and hit the green call button to initiate the call.
2. **Answering a Call:**
   - When you receive a call, your Apple Watch will vibrate and display the caller's name or number. Swipe up on the green phone icon to answer, or swipe down to decline.
   - If you're unable to answer at the moment, scroll down and tap *Send*

a Message to respond with a pre-set text or create a custom message.

3. **Using Speakerphone and Headphones:**
   - You can use the built-in speaker and microphone to talk directly from your watch. If you have Bluetooth headphones connected, the audio will automatically route to them.
   - To switch between audio outputs, tap the audio icon during the call and select your preferred device.
4. **Transferring Calls to iPhone:**
   - If you start a call on your Apple Watch but want to continue it on your iPhone, simply swipe up on the phone icon on your iPhone lock screen and tap *Touch to Return to*

Call. This will seamlessly transfer the call from your watch to your phone.

Sending Messages and Emails

Sending and receiving messages and emails from your Apple Watch is quick and convenient. Here's how to manage your communications efficiently:

1. **Sending Messages:**
    - Open the *Messages* app on your Apple Watch and tap *New Message*. Choose a contact from your list or tap the *Microphone* icon to dictate a new contact name.
    - Use voice dictation, Scribble, or the pre-set responses to compose your message. Tap *Send* when you're finished.

- For quick responses, you can use Smart Replies, which suggest context-aware responses based on the message content.

2. **Replying to Messages:**
    - When you receive a message, your watch will notify you with a tap. Raise your wrist to view the message. Scroll down to choose from quick replies or tap the *Microphone* icon to dictate a reply.
    - To reply using Scribble, tap the Scribble icon and use your finger to write letters on the screen. Your watch will recognize your handwriting and convert it to text.
3. **Composing and Sending Emails:**
    - Open the *Mail* app on your Apple Watch and tap *New Message*. Use dictation or Scribble to compose

your email. Select a recipient from your contacts or type a new email address.

- Tap *Send* to deliver your email. You can also use Smart Replies in the Mail app for quick responses to incoming emails.

4. **Customizing Notifications and Settings:**
    - Go to the *Watch* app on your iPhone, tap *Notifications*, and select *Messages* or *Mail* to customize how you receive notifications and alerts. You can choose to mirror your iPhone settings or set custom options for each app.

Calendar and Reminders Integration

Your Apple Watch integrates seamlessly with the Calendar and Reminders apps, keeping you organized and on top of your schedule.

1. **Viewing and Managing Calendar Events:**
   - Open the *Calendar* app on your watch to see your day's schedule. Use the Digital Crown to scroll through upcoming events.
   - Tap on an event to see more details, including location, participants, and notes. You can also use Siri to add new events, such as "Hey Siri, schedule a meeting for 3 PM tomorrow."
2. **Adding Events:**
   - To add a new event, press firmly on the screen within the *Calendar* app

and tap *New Event*. Use voice dictation to enter the event details, including title, date, and time.

- You can also invite contacts to events directly from your watch by adding participants during the event creation process.

3. **Setting Up Reminders:**
   - Open the *Reminders* app and tap *New Reminder*. Use voice dictation or Scribble to enter your reminder. You can assign reminders to specific lists, set due dates, and add notes.
   - To quickly set a reminder using Siri, say something like, "Remind me to buy groceries at 6 PM." Siri will add the reminder to your default list with the specified time.

4. **Managing Reminders:**
   - To mark a reminder as complete, open the *Reminders* app, scroll to the task, and tap on it. You can also snooze or delete reminders from your watch.
   - Use the *Watch* app on your iPhone to customize how reminders are displayed on your watch. This includes choosing which reminder lists to sync and setting notification preferences.
5. **Syncing and Sharing Calendars:**
   - The *Calendar* app on your Apple Watch syncs with the Calendar app on your iPhone. To share a calendar with others, open the *Calendar* app on your iPhone, select the calendar, and tap *Add Person*. Enter the email address of

the person you want to share with, and they will receive an invitation.

By mastering these productivity and communication features on your Apple Watch Series 10, you can efficiently manage your day-to-day tasks and stay connected, all from your wrist. Whether you're using Siri, making calls, sending messages, or organizing your schedule, the Series 10 enhances your productivity and keeps you in control, no matter where you are.

Media and Entertainment on Apple Watch Series 10

The Apple Watch Series 10 is not just a fitness and productivity tool; it also serves as a versatile media and entertainment device. Whether you want to listen to music, podcasts, or audiobooks, or stream from your favorite services, the Series 10 has you covered. This guide will provide detailed, step-by-step instructions for accessing and managing media on your Apple Watch, ensuring you get the most out of its entertainment capabilities.

Playing Music, Podcasts, and Audiobooks

The Apple Watch allows you to play music, podcasts, and audiobooks directly from your wrist, making it easy to enjoy your favorite content on the go. Here's how to set up and use these features:

1. **Playing Music:**
   - **Syncing Music to Your Watch:** To play music without your iPhone nearby, you need to sync songs to your Apple Watch. Open the *Watch* app on your iPhone, go to *My Watch*, and tap on *Music*. Select *Add Music* and choose playlists, albums, or songs to sync to your watch. Ensure your watch is charging while syncing, as this process may take some time.
   - **Playing Music Directly from Your Watch:** Once synced, open the *Music* app on your Apple Watch. Use the Digital Crown to scroll through your music library. Tap on a song or playlist to play it.

If you have Bluetooth headphones connected, the audio will automatically route through them.

  - **Using Siri to Play Music:** You can also ask Siri to play specific songs, artists, or playlists. For example, say, "Hey Siri, play my workout playlist," and Siri will start playing the requested music.

2. **Listening to Podcasts:**
    - **Syncing Podcasts to Your Watch:** Open the *Watch* app on your iPhone and tap *Podcasts*. Choose *Custom* to select specific podcasts to sync, or *Up Next* to automatically sync the latest episodes of your subscribed shows.
    - **Playing Podcasts on Your Watch:** Open the *Podcasts* app on your Apple Watch. You'll see a list

of available episodes. Tap on an episode to start playing it. You can control playback using the Digital Crown or the on-screen controls.

- **Using Siri for Podcasts:** Ask Siri to play a specific podcast or the latest episode of a subscribed show. For example, say, "Hey Siri, play the latest episode of *The Daily*."

3. **Enjoying Audiobooks:**
   - **Adding Audiobooks to Your Watch:** Open the *Watch* app on your iPhone, go to *Audiobooks*, and select *Add Audiobook*. You can choose from purchased audiobooks in your Apple Books library or from your Audible account if the app is installed on your watch.

- **Playing Audiobooks on Your Watch:** Open the *Audiobooks* app on your watch and tap on a title to start listening. The app will remember your place, so you can pick up right where you left off.
- **Using Siri for Audiobooks:** You can ask Siri to play a specific audiobook or to resume where you left off by saying, "Hey Siri, play my audiobook."

4. **Playback Controls:**
   - Use the Digital Crown to adjust the volume during playback. Tap the play/pause button to control playback, or use the skip forward and backward buttons to navigate through tracks, episodes, or chapters.

- To control playback from your iPhone, open the *Now Playing* screen on the watch, which will mirror what's playing on your iPhone. This is useful if you're using your phone to stream content but want to control it from your watch.

Streaming Services on Apple Watch

The Apple Watch Series 10 supports streaming from various services directly on the device. Here's how to set up and use streaming services for music and more:

1. **Apple Music and Apple Podcasts:**
    - **Streaming Music:** If you have an Apple Music subscription, you can stream songs and playlists directly on your watch without needing to

download them first. Open the *Music* app, browse through your library or the Apple Music catalog, and tap to play.

  - **Streaming Podcasts:** Open the *Podcasts* app and browse through the catalog. Tap on an episode to start streaming. Ensure your watch is connected to Wi-Fi or cellular for uninterrupted playback.

2. **Third-Party Music Services:**
   - **Spotify:** Download the Spotify app on your Apple Watch. You can use it to control playback from your phone or stream music directly if you have a Spotify Premium subscription. Open the app, select a playlist or song, and tap to play.

- **Pandora and Deezer:** These apps also support streaming directly from your watch if you have the necessary subscriptions. Install the app from the App Store on your watch, sign in, and start playing.

3. **Streaming Audiobooks:**
    - **Audible:** If you have the Audible app on your Apple Watch, you can stream audiobooks directly from the app. Open Audible, select a title from your library, and tap to stream. You can also download audiobooks to your watch for offline listening.
4. **Streaming Videos:**
    - While the Apple Watch is primarily designed for audio content, you can use apps like WatchTube to

stream short videos directly on the watch. This is useful for quick tutorials or entertainment clips but is not recommended for extended viewing due to the small screen size.

Managing Media Files

Managing your media files on the Apple Watch ensures that you have the content you need without taking up too much storage space. Here's how to effectively manage and organize your media:

1. **Checking Storage:**
    - Open the *Settings* app on your Apple Watch, go to *General*, and select *Storage*. Here, you can see how much space is available and

how much is being used by apps, music, podcasts, and other media.
    - This information helps you decide which content to keep on your watch and which to remove to free up space.

2. **Removing Media:**
    - **Music:** Open the *Watch* app on your iPhone, go to *Music*, and swipe left on a playlist or album to delete it from your watch.
    - **Podcasts:** Go to the *Podcasts* section in the *Watch* app, select the podcast you want to remove, and turn off *Show on Apple Watch*. This will remove all episodes of that podcast from your device.
    - **Audiobooks:** In the *Audiobooks* section of the *Watch* app, swipe left

on a title to delete it from your watch.

3. **Organizing Playlists and Albums:**
   - You can create specific playlists for different activities, such as workouts, relaxation, or commutes. Open the *Music* app on your iPhone, create a new playlist, and add songs or albums.
   - Sync these playlists to your watch by selecting them in the *Watch* app under *Music* and adding them to your sync list.
4. **Customizing Media Sync Settings:**
   - To manage how and when your media syncs to your watch, go to the *Watch* app on your iPhone, select *Music*, *Podcasts*, or *Audiobooks*, and customize your sync settings. You can choose to

sync only when your watch is charging or connected to Wi-Fi to save battery life.

5. **Using the Now Playing Screen:**
   - The *Now Playing* screen on your Apple Watch lets you control playback for any media playing on your watch or iPhone. Swipe up on the watch face to access the Control Center and tap *Now Playing* to see playback controls, volume adjustment, and track navigation.

By mastering these media and entertainment features on your Apple Watch Series 10, you can enjoy a seamless and immersive experience, whether you're listening to your favorite music, catching up on podcasts, or enjoying an engaging audiobook.

With the ability to manage and stream content directly from your wrist, your entertainment options are always just a tap away.

Connectivity and Settings on Apple Watch Series 10

The Apple Watch Series 10 is designed to keep you connected and in control of your digital life, whether you're using cellular data, Wi-Fi, or managing your device's settings for optimal performance. This guide provides detailed instructions on setting up cellular and Wi-Fi connectivity, managing networks, and adjusting settings to ensure your Apple Watch runs smoothly and efficiently.

Cellular and Wi-Fi Setup

Having a reliable connection on your Apple Watch allows you to make calls, send messages, use apps, and access the internet without your iPhone. Here's how to set up and configure both cellular and Wi-Fi on your Apple Watch Series 10:

1. **Setting Up Cellular Connectivity:**
   - **Check Compatibility:** Ensure that your Apple Watch Series 10 model supports cellular connectivity. You'll need a cellular-enabled model and a compatible cellular plan from your carrier.
   - **Pair Your Watch with iPhone:** Open the *Watch* app on your iPhone, go to *My Watch*, and tap *Cellular*. Tap *Set Up Cellular*, and follow the on-screen instructions to link your carrier plan with your Apple Watch. You may need to sign in to your carrier's account and confirm the plan details.
   - **Activate Cellular Service:** Once the setup is complete, your Apple Watch will be connected to your

cellular plan. You can check the status of your cellular connection by swiping up on the watch face to access the Control Center. Look for the cellular signal bars to confirm the connection.

- **Switch Between Cellular and Wi-Fi:** Your Apple Watch will automatically switch between Wi-Fi and cellular to save battery life. If Wi-Fi is available, it will prioritize that connection. If Wi-Fi is not available, it will use cellular data. You can manually control this by turning off Wi-Fi in the settings if you prefer to use cellular exclusively.

2. **Connecting to Wi-Fi Networks:**
   - **Automatic Wi-Fi Connection:** If your Apple Watch is paired with

your iPhone, it will automatically connect to any Wi-Fi network your iPhone has previously connected to. This is convenient because it eliminates the need to manually enter passwords on your watch.

- **Manually Connecting to Wi-Fi:** If you want to connect to a new Wi-Fi network directly from your Apple Watch, go to *Settings > Wi-Fi*, and select the desired network. Enter the password using Scribble or voice dictation. This is useful if your iPhone is not nearby or is turned off.
- **Checking Wi-Fi Status:** Swipe up on the watch face to access the Control Center, and look for the Wi-Fi icon. A blue Wi-Fi icon indicates a successful connection,

while a gray icon means the watch is not connected.

3. **Switching Between Networks:**
   - **Switching to Cellular Manually:** If you want to disconnect from a Wi-Fi network and use cellular data instead, go to *Settings* > *Wi-Fi* on your Apple Watch, and turn off Wi-Fi. This forces your watch to use cellular data.
   - **Switching Wi-Fi Networks:** To switch between Wi-Fi networks, go to *Settings* > *Wi-Fi*, tap the network you want to join, and enter the password if required. You can also forget networks that you no longer want your watch to connect to.

Managing Connections and Networks

Managing your Apple Watch's connections and networks is crucial for maintaining a stable connection and ensuring that your watch performs optimally. Here's how to manage and troubleshoot your connections:

1. **Viewing and Managing Network Connections:**
   - **Viewing Connected Networks:** Open the *Settings* app on your Apple Watch and go to *Wi-Fi* or *Cellular* to see the list of available and connected networks. You can view details such as signal strength and IP addresses for each network.
   - **Forgetting a Wi-Fi Network:** If you no longer want your Apple Watch to connect to a specific Wi-Fi network, go to *Settings* >

Wi-Fi, tap on the network name, and select *Forget This Network*. This will remove the network from your saved list.

2. **Managing Cellular Data Usage:**
   - **Viewing Data Usage:** Open the *Watch* app on your iPhone, go to *My Watch* > *Cellular*, and view your data usage. This is useful for monitoring your cellular data consumption and avoiding overage charges.
   - **Limiting Data Usage:** You can manage your data usage by turning off cellular data for specific apps. Go to *Settings* > *Cellular* on your Apple Watch and toggle off the apps you don't want to use cellular data.

3. **Troubleshooting Connection Issues:**
   - **Restarting Your Watch:** If you're experiencing connectivity issues, try restarting your Apple Watch. Press and hold the side button until the power off slider appears, then slide to power off. Press and hold the side button again to turn it back on.
   - **Resetting Network Settings:** If restarting doesn't resolve the issue, try resetting your network settings. Go to *Settings* > *General* > *Reset*, and select *Reset Network Settings*. This will remove all saved Wi-Fi networks, so you'll need to reconnect manually.
   - **Updating WatchOS:** Ensure your watch is running the latest

version of WatchOS. Go to the *Watch* app on your iPhone, select *General*, then *Software Update*. If an update is available, download and install it.

Adjusting Settings for Optimal Performance

Fine-tuning your Apple Watch settings can significantly improve performance and battery life. Here's how to adjust your settings for optimal use:

1. **Adjusting Display Settings:**
    - **Brightness and Text Size:** Go to *Settings > Display & Brightness* on your watch. Adjust the brightness slider to a comfortable level. You can also increase the text size for better readability.

- **Always-On Display:** If you have the Series 10, you can enable or disable the always-on display to save battery. Go to *Settings* > *Display & Brightness*, and toggle *Always On* on or off.

2. **Customizing Notifications:**
    - **Managing Notifications for Each App:** Open the *Watch* app on your iPhone, go to *Notifications*, and select each app to customize how notifications are delivered. You can choose to mirror your iPhone's settings or set custom options for each app.
    - **Enabling Do Not Disturb and Focus Modes:** Use Do Not Disturb or Focus modes to limit interruptions. Swipe up on the watch face to access the Control

Center, and tap the crescent moon icon for Do Not Disturb. For Focus modes, go to *Settings* > *Focus* and choose your preferred mode.

3. **Optimizing Battery Life:**
   - **Using Power Reserve Mode:** If your battery is running low, activate Power Reserve mode by pressing and holding the side button, then dragging the Power Reserve slider. This mode limits functionality to just displaying the time, preserving battery life.
   - **Managing Background App Refresh:** Go to the *Watch* app on your iPhone, select *General*, and tap *Background App Refresh*. Turn off the feature for apps that don't need to update frequently, reducing battery drain.

4. **Customizing Workout Settings:**
    - **Adjusting Workout Metrics:** Open the *Workout* app on your watch, tap the three dots icon next to a workout, and customize metrics like duration, distance, or calories burned. This helps tailor your workouts to your fitness goals.
    - **Optimizing GPS for Workouts:** If you use your watch for running or cycling, ensure that GPS is optimized for accuracy. Go to *Settings* > *Privacy* > *Location Services*, and set it to *While Using* for the Workout app.

By following these detailed instructions for setting up and managing connectivity and adjusting your Apple Watch settings, you can ensure that your device performs optimally and stays connected wherever you go. Whether you're using cellular data, connecting to Wi-Fi, or tweaking settings for better battery life, these tips will help you get the most out of your Apple Watch Series 10.

Apple Watch Customization

The Apple Watch Series 10 offers extensive customization options, allowing you to personalize your watch to match your style and preferences. From changing watch faces and complications to adjusting display settings and fine-tuning haptic feedback, you can make your watch truly your own. This guide provides detailed, step-by-step instructions on how to customize your Apple Watch for the best user experience.

Changing Watch Faces and Complications

The watch face is the main screen of your Apple Watch, and there are numerous styles to choose from, ranging from classic analog designs to vibrant, information-rich digital displays.

Here's how to change watch faces and customize complications:

1. **Changing Watch Faces:**
   - **Accessing the Watch Face Gallery:** To change your watch face directly on your Apple Watch, press firmly on the current watch face to enter the watch face gallery. Swipe left or right to browse through available faces. You can also access the gallery through the Watch app on your iPhone.
   - **Selecting a New Watch Face:** When you find a face you like, tap *Customize* if you want to adjust its settings or simply tap *Set* to make it your new watch face. You can also add a new face by swiping all the way to the right and tapping the *New* button (+).

- **Using the Watch App on iPhone:** Open the *Watch* app on your iPhone and go to the *Face Gallery* tab at the bottom. Browse through different categories such as *Infograph*, *California*, *Artist*, or *Modular Compact*. Tap on a face to see customization options and add it to your watch.

2. **Customizing Complications:**
   - **What Are Complications?** Complications are small widgets that display useful information such as weather, calendar events, activity rings, or battery life. They can be added to most watch faces, making it easy to view important data at a glance.
   - **Editing Complications on the Watch:** After choosing a watch

face, press firmly on the display and tap *Customize*. Swipe left to access the complications screen. Tap on a complication area, and use the Digital Crown to scroll through available options, such as Activity, Weather, Music, or custom apps you've installed.

- **Using the Watch App on iPhone:** In the *Watch* app, go to *My Watch > Watch Faces*, and select the face you want to customize. Tap a complication slot and choose from a list of available options. This method offers a broader view and more control over your selections compared to doing it directly on the watch.

3. **Creating and Managing Multiple Watch Faces:**
    - **Adding Multiple Faces:** You can create multiple watch faces for different occasions or needs. For example, you can have one face with work-related complications and another focused on fitness.
    - **Switching Between Faces:** Swipe left or right on the watch face to quickly switch between your saved faces. This feature is handy when you want to change the information displayed without going into the settings.
4. **Removing and Reordering Watch Faces:**
    - **Removing a Watch Face:** To delete a watch face, press firmly on the face, swipe up, and tap the

trash icon. This will remove it from your saved faces but won't delete it from the watch's library.

- **Reordering Faces:** In the *Watch* app on your iPhone, go to *My Watch > Watch Faces*. Tap and hold the three lines next to a face and drag it up or down to reorder your faces.

Adjusting Brightness and Display Settings

The display settings on your Apple Watch can be adjusted to improve readability and conserve battery life. Here's how to fine-tune these settings:

1. **Adjusting Brightness:**
    - **On the Apple Watch:** Go to *Settings > Display & Brightness.*

Use the sliders to increase or decrease the brightness. A lower brightness setting can help extend battery life, while a higher setting improves visibility in bright conditions.

- **Using the Watch App on iPhone:** Open the *Watch* app, go to *My Watch*, and select *Display & Brightness*. Adjust the brightness sliders to your preference.

2. **Enabling Always-On Display:**
    - The Series 10 supports an always-on display, which keeps the watch face visible even when your wrist is down. To enable or disable this feature, go to *Settings* > *Display & Brightness* > *Always On*. Toggle the switch to turn it on or off.

- You can also customize which information remains visible in always-on mode by selecting *Show Complications* and choosing which complications appear on the dimmed screen.

3. **Text Size and Bold Text:**
   - **Adjusting Text Size:** If you find the text on your watch difficult to read, go to *Settings* > *Display & Brightness* > *Text Size*. Use the Digital Crown to increase or decrease the text size.
   - **Enabling Bold Text:** For better readability, turn on *Bold Text* in the same menu. This will make all on-screen text appear thicker and more prominent.

4. **Toggling Wake Screen Settings:**
   - **Wake on Wrist Raise:** Your watch can wake the screen when you raise your wrist. Go to *Settings > Display & Brightness > Wake on Wrist Raise* to toggle this feature.
   - **Wake Duration:** Choose how long the display stays on after tapping it. Go to *Settings > Display & Brightness > Wake Duration* and select 15 seconds or 70 seconds, depending on your preference.

Customizing Haptic Feedback and Sounds

The Apple Watch uses haptic feedback and sound alerts to notify you of calls, messages, and other alerts. You can adjust these settings to suit your needs:

1. **Customizing Haptic Feedback:**
   - **Adjusting Haptic Intensity:** Go to *Settings* > *Sounds & Haptics* on your Apple Watch. Under *Haptic Strength*, use the slider to increase or decrease the intensity of the vibrations. A stronger setting makes it easier to notice notifications.
   - **Enabling Prominent Haptics:** Turn on *Prominent Haptics* to add an extra pre-vibration before common alerts. This feature helps ensure you don't miss important notifications.
2. **Customizing Sound Alerts:**
   - **Adjusting Volume:** In *Settings* > *Sounds & Haptics*, use the *Alert Volume* slider to set the desired loudness for alerts and

notifications. You can also change this setting in the *Watch* app on your iPhone under *Sounds & Haptics*.

- **Turning On/Off Sound Alerts:** If you prefer not to have sound alerts, you can mute them by toggling the *Silent Mode* switch in the *Control Center*. Swipe up on the watch face to access the Control Center and tap the bell icon to enable or disable silent mode.

3. **Enabling/Disabling Taptic Time:**
   - The Taptic Time feature allows you to feel the time through haptic feedback instead of seeing it. To enable this, go to *Settings > Clock > Taptic Time* and choose a pattern such as *Digits* or *Terse*. You can then touch and hold two

fingers on the watch face to have the time tapped out on your wrist.

4. **Using Theater Mode:**
    - Theater Mode prevents the watch screen from lighting up with wrist movements and mutes notifications. This is useful in settings like movie theaters or meetings. To enable it, swipe up to access the Control Center and tap the Theater Mode icon (two masks). The watch will remain dark and only provide haptic feedback for notifications.
5. **Managing Notification Settings:**
    - Go to *Settings* > *Notifications* on your watch to manage how you receive notifications. You can choose to have notifications mirrored from your iPhone or set

custom notifications for each app. This allows you to prioritize which alerts use haptic feedback and sound.

By following these detailed steps, you can personalize your Apple Watch Series 10 to fit your style and preferences perfectly. Whether it's changing watch faces, adjusting display settings, or customizing haptic feedback, these options allow you to create a user experience that's tailored to you. Enjoy exploring the many ways you can make your Apple Watch truly your own!

Advanced Features of Apple Watch Series 10

The Apple Watch Series 10 introduces several advanced features that enhance its usability, health tracking capabilities, and user experience. From the innovative magnetic band attachment system to voice isolation for clearer calls and comprehensive health data management, these features make the watch a more powerful tool for users. This guide explains each of these advanced features with step-by-step instructions to help you get the most out of your Apple Watch.

Using the New Magnetic Band Attachment System

The new magnetic band attachment system in the Apple Watch Series 10 is designed to provide a more convenient and secure way to change watch bands. This system eliminates the need for traditional clasps or buckles, allowing for easy customization and a comfortable fit.

1. **Understanding the Magnetic Band System:**
   - The magnetic band attachment system uses powerful magnets embedded in the watch and the band, which align perfectly to secure the band in place. This design not only provides a seamless look but also ensures that the band remains securely attached during various activities.
2. **Attaching a Magnetic Band:**
   - To attach a magnetic band, hold the band near the watch body where the connectors are located. The magnets will automatically align the band into place. Ensure

both ends of the band click securely.

- Gently pull on the band to confirm that it is firmly attached. If it feels loose, realign the band to ensure the magnets are fully engaged.

3. **Removing the Band:**
    - To remove the magnetic band, simply hold one end of the band and pull it away from the watch body with a firm yet gentle motion. The magnets will release, allowing you to detach the band easily.
    - Avoid pulling the band too forcefully, as this could potentially damage the connectors.
4. **Benefits of the Magnetic Band System:**
    - The magnetic band attachment system is particularly useful for

users who like to switch bands frequently. It provides a quick and hassle-free way to change the look and feel of your watch to match different occasions or activities.

- It also enhances comfort, as the magnetic system ensures a perfect fit without the need for adjusting clasps or buckles.

Voice Isolation for Calls

Voice isolation is a feature on the Apple Watch Series 10 that enhances call clarity by minimizing background noise and focusing on your voice. This is especially useful in noisy environments, ensuring that the person on the other end can hear you clearly.

1. **Enabling Voice Isolation:**
    - During a phone call, swipe up on the call interface to access the Control Center.
    - Tap the *Microphone Mode* button and select *Voice Isolation*. This will activate the feature, filtering out ambient noise and enhancing your voice quality.
2. **Testing Voice Isolation:**
    - To test the effectiveness of voice isolation, make a call in a noisy environment such as a cafe or a busy street. Notice how the watch reduces background sounds and enhances your voice, making the conversation clearer for the person on the other end.
    - You can also compare the call quality by switching between

different microphone modes (Standard, Wide Spectrum, and Voice Isolation) to see which works best for your current environment.

3. **Using Voice Isolation with Other Apps:**
   - Voice isolation isn't limited to phone calls. You can also use it with apps like FaceTime or any other communication app that supports microphone mode selection. This ensures consistent audio quality across different platforms.
4. **Deactivating Voice Isolation:**
   - To turn off voice isolation, repeat the steps above and select *Standard* or *Wide Spectrum* mode. This will return the microphone settings to their default state.

Managing Sleep and Breathing Data

The Apple Watch Series 10 offers advanced sleep and breathing data tracking features that help you monitor your overall wellness. These features provide insights into your sleep patterns and respiratory health, making it easier to maintain a healthy lifestyle.

1. **Setting Up Sleep Tracking:**
    - Open the *Health* app on your iPhone and tap *Set Up Sleep*. Follow the on-screen instructions to set your desired sleep schedule, bedtime, and wake-up time.
    - Enable *Sleep Mode* on your Apple Watch by going to *Settings* > *Sleep* and toggling *Sleep Mode* on. This will dim the display and activate Do Not Disturb during your scheduled sleep hours.

2. **Tracking Your Sleep:**
   - Wear your Apple Watch to bed. The watch will automatically track your sleep stages, such as light sleep, deep sleep, and REM, and monitor your breathing rate throughout the night.
   - In the morning, open the *Sleep* app on your watch or the *Health* app on your iPhone to view a detailed report of your sleep duration, stages, and any disturbances.
3. **Monitoring Breathing Data:**
   - The watch tracks your respiratory rate, which is the number of breaths you take per minute during sleep. This data can indicate changes in your respiratory health.
   - To view your breathing data, open the *Health* app on your iPhone and

go to *Respiratory*. You can see a graph of your average respiratory rate over time, along with any significant variations.

4. **Setting Breathing Reminders:**
   - To promote relaxation and mindful breathing, set up reminders using the *Breathe* app on your watch. Open the *Breathe* app and set the duration and frequency of your breathing sessions.
   - During a breathing session, the watch will guide you through deep breathing exercises, helping reduce stress and improve focus.
5. **Reviewing Trends and Insights:**
   - The *Health* app provides a comprehensive view of your sleep and breathing data over time. You can see trends and insights, such as

how consistent your sleep schedule is or how your respiratory rate changes with your activity levels.

  - Use this information to make adjustments to your sleep habits and improve your overall health.

Integrating with Apple Health Ecosystem

The Apple Watch integrates seamlessly with the Apple Health ecosystem, allowing you to consolidate and analyze all your health data in one place. This integration enables you to track various health metrics and share data with healthcare providers.

1. **Syncing Data with the Health App:**
   - Open the *Watch* app on your iPhone, go to *My Watch* > *Health*, and ensure that all health data

categories you want to track are enabled. This includes metrics like heart rate, respiratory rate, and sleep data.

- The watch will automatically sync this data with the *Health* app, where you can view it in the *Health Data*section.

2. **Viewing and Analyzing Health Data:**
   - Open the *Health* app on your iPhone and go to *Summary* or *Health Data*. You can view individual metrics such as heart rate, blood oxygen levels, and activity data.
   - Use the *Trends* feature to see how your metrics have changed over time. This can help you identify patterns and make informed

decisions about your health and fitness routine.

3. **Sharing Health Data with Providers:**
    - If you need to share your health data with a healthcare provider, go to the *Health* app and select the *Share* tab. Choose which data to share and with whom. This feature is useful for remote consultations and ongoing health monitoring.
4. **Integrating Third-Party Apps:**
    - You can connect third-party health and fitness apps to the Apple Health ecosystem. Go to the *Health* app, tap *Sources*, and select the app you want to integrate. Ensure that all relevant data categories are enabled for syncing.

    - Apps like MyFitnessPal, Strava, and Sleep Cycle can provide additional insights and help you achieve your fitness and health goals.

5. **Setting Up Health Notifications:**
    - Go to *Health > Health Checklist* in the *Health* app to enable health-related notifications. You can set up alerts for irregular heart rhythms, high or low heart rate, and other health metrics.
    - These notifications can alert you to potential health issues, helping you take action before they become serious.

By mastering these advanced features, you can optimize your Apple Watch Series 10 experience and leverage its powerful capabilities to improve your health and communication. Whether you're using the new magnetic band attachment system, enhancing call quality with voice isolation, or integrating your health data, the Series 10 offers a comprehensive suite of tools to support your lifestyle.

Troubleshooting and Support for Apple Watch Series 10

The Apple Watch Series 10 is a sophisticated device, but like any technology, it can sometimes experience issues. Whether you're facing connectivity problems, performance lags, or difficulty syncing with your iPhone, understanding common troubleshooting steps can save time and frustration. This guide provides solutions for frequent problems, instructions for resetting and restoring your Apple Watch, and information on how to contact Apple Support for additional help.

Common Issues and Solutions

1. **Battery Draining Quickly:**
   - If you notice that your Apple Watch's battery is depleting faster than usual, try reducing the screen

brightness and disabling the *Always-On Display*. Go to *Settings > Display & Brightness* and adjust the brightness slider. To turn off the Always-On Display, go to *Settings > Display & Brightness > Always On* and toggle it off.

   - Disable background app refresh for apps that don't need to update continuously. Open the *Watch* app on your iPhone, go to *General > Background App Refresh*, and toggle off unnecessary apps.

2. **Watch Not Pairing with iPhone:**
   - Ensure that both devices are updated to the latest software. If the issue persists, reset the network settings on your iPhone by going to *Settings > General >*

Reset > Reset Network Settings. Then try pairing the devices again.

  - Restart both your iPhone and Apple Watch. Press and hold the side button on your Apple Watch until the power off slider appears, then turn it off. Do the same on your iPhone. After a few seconds, turn both devices back on and try pairing again.

3. **App Crashes or Freezes:**
   - If an app on your Apple Watch is crashing or freezing, force close it by pressing and holding the side button until the power off slider appears. Release the side button, then press and hold the Digital Crown until the app closes.
   - Restart your Apple Watch to clear any lingering issues. If the problem

continues, try uninstalling and reinstalling the app through the *Watch* app on your iPhone.

4. **Connectivity Issues (Wi-Fi/Cellular):**
   - Check that Wi-Fi and cellular are enabled on your watch. Go to *Settings > Wi-Fi* and ensure it is turned on. For cellular, open the *Control Center* by swiping up and make sure the cellular icon is active.
   - If the issue persists, reset the network settings on your Apple Watch. Go to *Settings > General > Reset > Reset Network Settings*. This will remove all saved Wi-Fi networks, so you'll need to reconnect manually.

Resetting and Restoring Your Apple Watch

If your Apple Watch is still experiencing problems after trying basic troubleshooting steps, you may need to reset or restore it. This process can resolve persistent software issues or prepare the watch for a new user.

1. **Soft Reset (Restarting):**
   - Press and hold the side button until the power off slider appears. Drag the slider to turn off the watch. To turn it back on, press and hold the side button again until the Apple logo appears.
2. **Force Restart:**
   - If your watch is unresponsive, press and hold both the Digital Crown and the side button simultaneously for at least 10

seconds until the Apple logo appears. This should only be done if a normal restart doesn't work.

3. **Factory Reset:**
    - Open the *Settings* app on your Apple Watch, go to *General* > *Reset*, and tap *Erase All Content and Settings*. Confirm the action, and your watch will reset to factory settings.
    - You can also perform a factory reset through the *Watch* app on your iPhone. Go to *General* > *Reset*, and select *Erase Apple Watch Content and Settings*. This will unpair the watch from your iPhone and reset it.
4. **Restoring from Backup:**
    - After resetting your watch, you can restore it from a previous backup.

During the setup process, when prompted, choose *Restore from Backup* and select the most recent backup from the list. This will restore your apps, settings, and data.

Contacting Apple Support

If the above troubleshooting steps don't resolve your issue, contacting Apple Support is the next step. Here's how you can get in touch:

1. **Apple Support Website:**
   - Visit support.apple.com for troubleshooting guides, user manuals, and community forums where you can find solutions to common problems. You can also schedule a repair or chat with an

Apple Support representative directly from the website.

2. **Apple Support Contacts:**
   - **U.S. Support Number:** 1-800-MY-APPLE (1-800-692-7753)
   - **International Support:** For international support numbers, visit Apple's Contact Page to find the contact information specific to your country or region.
3. **Apple Support App:**
   - Download the *Apple Support* app from the App Store. It allows you to access personalized support, schedule repairs, and chat with a support agent directly from your iPhone or iPad.

4. **Visit an Apple Store:**
   - If you prefer in-person assistance, you can visit your nearest Apple Store. It's recommended to schedule a Genius Bar appointment beforehand, which you can do through the *Apple Support* app or Apple's website.

By following these troubleshooting steps and contacting Apple Support when necessary, you can effectively resolve most issues with your Apple Watch Series 10. This ensures that your device continues to operate smoothly and reliably, providing you with the best possible experience.

Appendices for Apple Watch Series 10 User Guide

The appendices section of the Apple Watch Series 10 user guide provides essential information about compatible accessories, legal and warranty details, as well as frequently asked questions and user tips. This section aims to enhance your experience with the device by providing easy access to additional resources and support.

List of Compatible Accessories

1. **Watch Bands:**
   - The Apple Watch Series 10 is compatible with a wide range of watch bands from previous Apple Watch models, including Series 4 through Series 9. This includes the

Sport Band, Solo Loop, Leather Link, and Milanese Loop.

- The new magnetic band system introduced with the Series 10 is also backward compatible with previous models, allowing you to use existing bands while enjoying the new magnetic attachment feature.

2. **Chargers and Docks:**
    - The Series 10 supports the new fast-charging magnetic USB-C cable that comes with the watch. It is also compatible with older Apple Watch charging cables, although these may not support fast charging.
    - Charging docks and stands from brands like Belkin, Nomad, and Mophie are compatible, provided

they support the magnetic charging puck designed for Apple Watch.

3. **Screen Protectors and Cases:**
   - To protect the display, screen protectors from companies like ZAGG, OtterBox, and Spigen are designed to fit the Series 10's screen dimensions. Ensure the protector is specifically made for the 45mm or 49mm size, depending on your watch model.
   - Protective cases are available from brands such as Catalyst and RhinoShield, offering impact resistance and water protection.
4. **Third-Party Apps and Fitness Accessories:**
   - The Apple Watch Series 10 supports a variety of third-party fitness accessories like heart rate

monitors, bike sensors, and gym equipment. Apps like Strava, Nike Run Club, and MyFitnessPal can integrate with these accessories to provide more detailed workout data.

- Smart straps that add additional functionality, such as extra battery life or sensors, can be attached using the traditional strap connectors, ensuring they work seamlessly with the Apple Watch.

Legal and Warranty Information

1. **Apple Watch Warranty:**
    - The Apple Watch Series 10 comes with a limited one-year warranty, which covers hardware defects and manufacturing issues. This warranty can be extended with the

purchase of AppleCare+, which adds two years of coverage and includes accidental damage protection.
    - For full details on the warranty, visit support.apple.com/warranty.
2. **AppleCare+ Coverage:**
    - AppleCare+ provides coverage for up to two incidents of accidental damage every 12 months, subject to a service fee. It also includes priority access to technical support and battery service.
    - For more information or to purchase AppleCare+, visit support.apple.com/applecare.
3. **Regulatory Compliance:**
    - The Apple Watch Series 10 complies with all applicable international standards for safety

and environmental impact, including FCC, CE, and RoHS certifications. Specific information about these certifications can be found in the settings of your Apple Watch under *General* > *Regulatory*.

4. **Software License Agreement:**
   - The use of the Apple Watch Series 10 is subject to Apple's software license agreement, which includes terms and conditions regarding the use of WatchOS. For the full agreement, visit apple.com/legal/sla.

FAQs and User Tips

1. **How Do I Pair My Apple Watch with a New iPhone?**

   - To pair your Apple Watch with a new iPhone, first unpair it from your old iPhone using the *Watch* app. Then, turn on your new iPhone and place it near the watch. Follow the on-screen instructions to complete the pairing process. Make sure your new iPhone has a backup of your old iPhone to restore all your data.
2. **How Can I Extend the Battery Life of My Apple Watch?**
   - To extend battery life, consider lowering the screen brightness, turning off the Always-On Display, and disabling background app refresh for non-essential apps. Using Power Reserve mode can also help preserve battery life in low-battery situations.

3. **How Do I Update the WatchOS?**
    - To update WatchOS, ensure your watch is connected to Wi-Fi and placed on its charger. Open the *Watch* app on your iPhone, go to *General > Software Update*, and follow the prompts to download and install the latest version.
4. **How Can I Use My Apple Watch Without My iPhone Nearby?**
    - If you have a cellular model, you can use the watch independently for calls, messages, and internet access. For Wi-Fi models, you can use it within the range of a known Wi-Fi network. Offline features like music playback and fitness tracking are always available.
5. **How Do I Reset My Apple Watch to Factory Settings?**

- To reset your watch, go to *Settings > General > Reset > Erase All Content and Settings*. This will remove all data and settings from the watch, returning it to its factory state.

6. **What Should I Do if My Apple Watch Gets Wet?**
   - The Series 10 is water-resistant up to 50 meters. If it gets wet, you can use the Water Lock feature to expel water from the speaker. Turn the Digital Crown until you see a series of sounds and vibrations ejecting water from the speaker.
7. **Tips for Maximizing Apple Watch Performance:**
   - Regularly restart your Apple Watch to keep it running smoothly.

- Clear unnecessary apps and data to free up storage space.
- Keep your watch and apps updated to the latest versions to ensure compatibility and performance.

By following these guidelines and utilizing the available support resources, you can enjoy a seamless and enriched experience with your Apple Watch Series 10. For further assistance, visit support.apple.com or contact Apple Support directly.

Printed in Great Britain
by Amazon

56722028R00090